Text by Mary Joslin
Illustrations copyright © 2020 Kristina Swarner
This edition copyright © 2020 Lion Hudson IP Limited

Published by
Lion Hudson Limited
Wilkinson House, Jordan Hill Business Park,
Banbury Road, Oxford OX2 8DR, England
www.lionhudson.com

ISBN 978 0 7459 7750 8 (Hardback)
ISBN 978 0 7459 7751 5 (Paperback)

First edition hardback 2020
First edition paperback 2020

A catalogue record for this book is available from the British Library

Printed and bound in China, June 2020, LH54

The Gift of
Christmas

THE BOY WHO BLESSED THE WORLD

Retold by Mary Joslin
Illustrated by Kristina Swarner

LION
CHILDREN'S

ANY YEARS AGO, in the town of Nazareth, God sent an angel-messenger to a young woman called Mary.

"Peace be with you!" said the angel. "You are truly blessed."

Mary was troubled by these words.

"Don't be afraid," the angel said. "You will give birth to a son, and you will name him 'Jesus'. He is the promised one and will bring God's blessing to all people. He is God's gift to all the earth."

"How can I have a baby? I am not yet married."

"God's power will wrap around you and fill you. He will make it possible," the angel replied.

The angel's words took her breath away. Mary was filled with awe.

"May it happen as you have said."

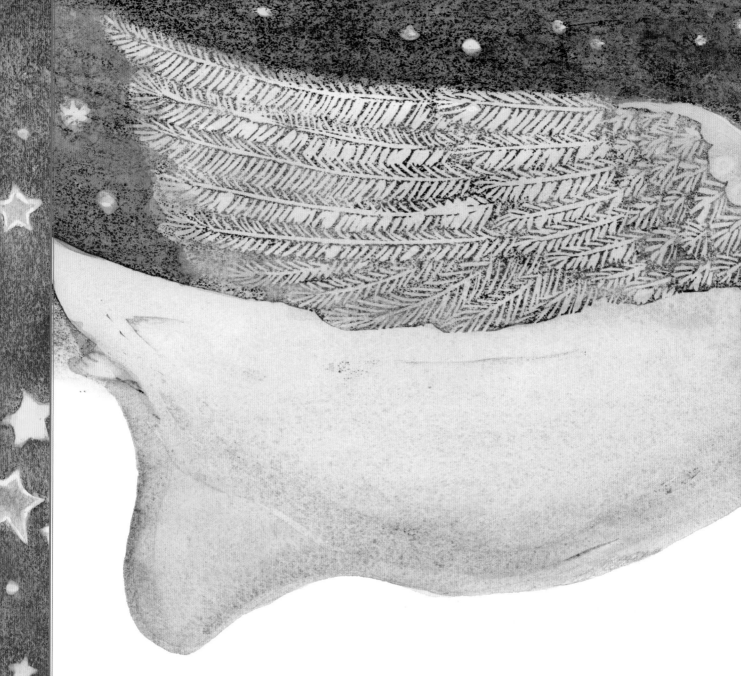

Mary was engaged to marry a carpenter named Joseph. When she whispered to him that she was pregnant, Joseph was dismayed.

"How can I marry her if she is expecting someone else's baby?" he thought sadly.

He made plans to quietly break their engagement. As he cared for her, he didn't want to publicly disgrace Mary.

While he was thinking about this, God sent an angel to him in a dream.

"Joseph, do not be afraid to take Mary as your wife," the angel said. "This child is a gift from God and He has chosen you to take care of them both."

At that time, Caesar Augustus ruled the mighty Roman empire. He demanded that all the people of his empire be counted. He wanted to collect taxes from each and every one of them. Everyone was told to have their names listed in their family's hometown.

So Joseph, with Mary, set off on the long journey south to Bethlehem.

They went to register there as husband and wife.

People had poured into the town of Bethlehem from far and wide to register.

As Mary arrived with Joseph, the time came for her baby to be born.

"We have come so far," she cried, "yet there is nowhere for us to stay. Whatever shall we do?"

"Don't worry," Joseph reassured her, "there is a warm, dry stable where we can shelter."

There among the animals, amidst the dirt and noise, Jesus came into the world as God's gift to all people.

Mary and Joseph welcomed him with loving arms. They wrapped him warmly in swaddling cloths and laid him in the animal's manger.

That night, on the hillsides sloping down from Bethlehem, shepherds were out looking after their flocks.

They sat in the cold night air, listening for the sounds of danger… the sniffing of prowling animals, the stealthy footsteps of thieves and robbers.

In a sudden blaze of brightness, a glorious angel appeared and the beauty and majesty of God shone over them.

They were terrified.

"Don't be afraid! I am here with good news for you," the angel said. "God has blessed the earth with his most precious gift. His Son Jesus has come!

"This very day in Bethlehem your Saviour was born. You will find him wrapped in strips of cloth and lying in a manger."

A mighty gathering of heaven's angels swiftly filled the night skies, singing praises to God: "Glory to God in the highest heaven, and peace on earth."

hen the angels were gone. Darkness and silence enveloped the skies once more. The amazed shepherds stared at one another.

"Can the Saviour really be here?" they asked each other. "God's promised king has come to earth! Shall we go and see?"

Still shaking, they hurried away to Bethlehem to find him.

In the animal's lowly stable they found Mary and the baby, just as the angel had said.

The shepherds gazed at Jesus in wonder. They described the song filled skies and the angels telling of how this baby would bring God's blessing to all people everywhere, for all time.

Soon after Jesus was born, three wise men from the east, who had studied the stars, journeyed across deserts and over the mountains.

They had discovered a bright new star in the night sky and were following it. They believed it would lead them to a new king.

The star led them to Jerusalem and the palace of cruel King Herod.

When Herod heard that they were looking for a newborn king he was deeply disturbed.

He called them to a secret meeting. "Tell me all about the star you are following," he said.

The wise men told him what they knew and when the star had first appeared.

"The holy books of our people tell us that a king will be born in Bethlehem," Herod told them. "Go! Look for this 'king'. When you have found him, return and tell me so I may worship him too."

As they rode on to Bethlehem, the star shone clearly ahead
of the three wise men. Finally it rested over one house.
There they found Mary, and her little boy Jesus.

The noble visitors fell to their knees and bowed their heads before this child, Jesus. They presented the family with treasures from their own lands: rich gifts of gold, frankincense, and myrrh.

Here, they believed, was a new king... *the* king for all nations of the world.

The wise men did not return to Herod in Jerusalem.

An angel advised them to travel home by a different road.

Joseph, too, was warned by an angel about cruel King Herod.

"Herod will be looking for Jesus in order to harm him. Leave quickly! Take your family to safety."

Leaving home, friends, and family, they fled to Egypt to protect Jesus.

Many years later, Jesus himself would show that he was indeed God's precious gift to the world. The baby king became the gift of Christmas, for all time.